SONNETS OF DARK L

SONETOS DEL AMOR OSCURO

Federico García Lorca

Federico García Lorca in 1914. Photographer unknown. Found in the University of Granada in 2007, student file.

∞ Editorial Anticuario ∞

Title: Sonnets of Dark Love
SONETOS DEL AMOR OSCURO
Translation into English
by Mar Escribano
Front cover: Darius M.G
Editor: Ariana M.G
ISBN: 9781717119896
Title ID: 8364978
Revised Edition: 2021
London, United Kingdom

Sonnets of Dark Love by Federico Garcia Lorca (1898-1936) have been translated into English by Mar Escribano. These poems were written in 1935, but were not published until after his death by the ABC Spanish newspaper on the 17th of March 1984, (clandestine editions were released before this date). This bilingual edition includes vintage images to get a better understanding of the romantic love he had for Ramirez de Lucas, together with explanations and comments for each sonnet. Lorca did not go to Mexico on exile (despite warnings that he may be killed) because Ramirez de Lucas' family refused him permission to travel with Lorca abroad. Ramirez de Lucas was under 21, and in Spain, at the time, you could not legally travel without parental permission.

SONETOS DEL AMOR OSCURO

SONNETS OF DARK LOVE

Federico García Lorca.

Soneto de la guirnalda de rosas

¡Esa guirnalda! ¡pronto! ¡que me muero!
¡Teje deprisa! ¡canta! ¡gime! ¡canta!
Que la sombra me enturbia la garganta
Y otra vez viene y mil la luz de Enero.

Entre lo que me quieres y te quiero,
Aire de estrellas y temblor de planta,
Espesura de anémonas levanta
Con oscuro gemir un año entero.

Goza el fresco paisaje de mi herida,
Quiebra juncos y arroyos delicados.
Bebe en muslo de miel sangre vertida.

Pero ¡pronto! Que unidos, enlazados,
Boca rota de amor y alma mórbida,
El tiempo nos encuentre destrozados.

Sonnet of the Garland of Roses

That garland! Quick! I am dying!
Weave it now! Sing! Moan! Sing!
For shadows my throat are clouding.
Once again January's light coming.

Wind of stars and plants trembling
Lie between our loving,
A dense mass of anemones rising.
Dark moaning for an entire year.

Have pleasure in my fresh wound!
Break apart my reeds and delicate rivulets!
Drink from my thigh my pouring blood.

But be quick! United and entwined
With our love-broken mouths and frayed souls
Time will find us destroyed.

Comments on the Sonnet, the Garland of Roses

The name of Federico Garcia Lorca's lover, Juan Ramirez de Lucas, emerged after 70 years of Lorca's death. Before Ramirez's death in 2010, he handed his sister a box containing mementoes of his and Lorca's yearlong passionate relationship. This piece of news spread quickly among literary and historical communities across the world. The box, which is still kept in a safety box, revealed that Lorca and 19-year-old Ramirez de Lucas had planned to go to Mexico together after falling in love in Madrid. Ramirez de Lucas was studying public administration and theatre in Madrid, and wanted to go to Mexico with Lorca, but he was too young. According to the Spanish law at the time, you needed your parents' permission to travel if you were under 21 years of age. Ramirez went back to his hometown, Albacete, days before the Spanish Civil War broke out, in an attempt to persuade his parents, but he was never given permission. Meanwhile, Lorca had gone to his birthplace, Granada, where he sought refuge in the house of his friends, the Rosales family.

In this first Sonnet, Garland of Roses, Lorca wrote the verse: 'con oscuro gemir un año entero' (dark moaning for an entire year), which reveals that their passionate relationship lasted for a year. 'Gemir' in Spanish can be translated into English as moaning, but also groaning. Both moaning and groaning can mean to utter noises of pain or grief. However, moaning is more so used to indicate a sound expressive of pleasure, whereas groaning is more often related to a sound made due to pain or distress. 'Gemir' in Spanish is a sound uttered during a sexual act (with the same connotations that 'moaning' has in English). Therefore 'moaning' is the preferable word in its translation into English.

It is important to understand the significance of the adjective OSCURO (DARK) and how this adjective is repeated in most of the sonnets; for example, 'oscuro gemir' (dark moaning). In Lorca's sonnets, dark does not mean with little or no light. It does not mean sad or without hope and it does not mean evil or threatening. For Lorca, dark (oscuro) implies sensual secrets. The word 'obscure' also exists in English and it does mean dark with certain connotations of occulted and recondite, but the image of obscure in an English native speaker's mind is more of something not discovered, not known or uncertain, not clearly expressed. Therefore, it doesn't serve its purpose into this translation.

Soneto de la dulce queja

Tengo miedo de perder la maravilla
De tus ojos de estatua y el acento
Que me pone de noche en la mejilla
La solitaria rosa de tu aliento.

Tengo pena de ser en esta orilla
Tronco sin ramas, y lo que más siento
Es no tener la flor, pulpa o arcilla,
Para el gusano de mi sufrimiento.

Si tú eres el tesoro oculto mío,
Si eres mi cruz y mi dolor mojado,
Si soy el perro de tu señorío.

No me dejes perder lo que he ganado
Y decora las aguas de tu río
Con hojas de mi otoño enajenado.

Sonnet of the Sweet Lament

I fear to lose the marvellous sight
Of your sculpted eyes; and the cadence
Of the solitary rose of your breath
Swinging on my cheek, at night.

I am sad to be on this shoreline,
Like a limbless tree; and what I fear the most
Is not having for my worm of agony
Flowers, wood pulp or potter's clay.

If you are my hidden treasure,
If you are my cross and wet ache
If I am the dog of your manor

Don't let me lose what I've won
And adorn the waters of your river
With the leaves of my estranged autumn.

Comments on the Sonnet of the Sweet Lament

Who was Juan Ramirez de Lucas? He was born in Albacete in 1917 and died in Madrid in 2010. He didn't end up going to Mexico with Lorca, but he did end up being a famous Spanish writer and a well-known critic of Spanish art. Lorca most likely wrote his Sonnets of Dark Love and his passionate verses to Ramirez de Lucas. It is thought that Ramirez was the source of inspiration for at least some of Lorca's poems, as inside the box of mementoes that Ramirez had kept, there are three items, which prove the relationship he had with Lorca. These three items are an unpublished poem, a letter, and a manuscript, all well kept inside a safety box. In the letter that Lorca wrote to Juan Ramirez de Lucas, he addresses his lover as "Juanito" and describes him as "The young blonde man from Albacete".

The family of Ramirez was conservative and had been appalled by their son's request to go to Mexico with Garcia Lorca. They refused him permission to travel, threatening to send him to the Guardia Civil. In the letter that Lorca wrote to him, Lorca told him to be patient and that it was important to remain close to his family. "Conmigo cuenta siempre. Yo soy tu mejor amigo y que te pide que seas 'político' y no dejes que el río te lleve." (Count on me always. I am your best friend and I ask you to be 'political' and not allow yourself to be washed along by the river (of fate). This letter was published by El Pais newspaper on the 5th of October 2014.

A handwriting expert has reviewed the poem, the letter and the manuscript, declaring them all to have been written by Garcia Lorca.

The Spanish author, Francisco Reina, who saw some of the contents of the box, said this proved the sonnets were addressed to Ramirez rather than to a previous Lorca lover, the football player Rafael Rodriguez. It then becomes evident that Lorca only stayed in the Rosales family residence to wait for Ramirez, but Granada was in the hands of General Francisco Franco, a fascist, whose death squads targeted Lorca.

Ramirez then joined the volunteer Blue Division to fight for Hitler against the Russians in an attempt to give himself the necessary credentials to survive in Franco's Spain. When he returned to Spain he became an art critic for many years, working for several magazines: 'Arquitectura' (Madrid), for ABC and Cemento Bilbao. Six of his books were published. He also won several prizes in architecture from the College of Architects of Madrid and Bulgaria.

Regarding his private life, we know very little. He was the lover of Lorca but kept his relationship secret, refusing to answer questions or talk about his personal life. The last verses of the sonnet of Sweet Lament, "adorn the waters of your river with the leaves of my estranged autumn" seem to be premonitory; in the river of the lover's life (the river of his fate), the memory of Lorca will remain in the form of floating leaves; leaves that have fallen from his 'limbless tree', which could symbolise the corpse of Lorca, still not found.

Llagas de amor

Esta luz, este fuego que devora.
Este paisaje gris que me rodea.
Este dolor por una sola idea.
Esta angustia de cielo, mundo y hora.

Este llanto de sangre que decora
Lira sin pulso ya, lúbrica tea.
Este peso del mar que me golpea.
Este alacrán que por mi pecho mora.

Son guirnalda de amor, cama de herido,
Donde sin sueño, sueño tu presencia
Entre las ruinas de mi pecho hundido.

Y aunque busco la cumbre de prudencia
Me da tu corazón valle tendido
Con cicuta y pasión de amarga ciencia.

Wounds of Love

This light, this devouring fire,
This grey landscape surrounding me,
This sorrow centred around one idea
This anguish of sky, earth and time.

This weeping of blood that adorns
A pulseless lyre, a lusty torch.
This weight of the sea that clobbers
This scorpion dwelling inside me.

They are a garland of love and a sickbed
Where I lie awake, dreaming of your presence
Among the ruins of my downcast heart.

Though looking for the pinnacle of prudence
Your heart gives me a laying valley.
With the poison and passion of the bitter reasoning.

Comments on the Sonnet of the Wounds of Love

I was strongly inclined to translate the title of this sonnet not with the word 'wounds', but with more powerful words such as 'injuries', 'cuts' or even 'ulcers', as wounds is 'heridas' in Spanish but the original title is with the word 'llagas'. Llagas are not simple wounds, llagas are deep wounds, sores, and deep cuts where the incision is deeper. This is the problem when translating Lorca. His words have stronger feelings in the original Spanish and, sometimes, this power diminishes when translated into English; the sentiment is not as strong.

Phrases such as 'devouring fire' and 'weeping of blood' make this a very sensual and erotic sonnet, especially in Spanish language. The 'pulseless lyre' is a lyre without pulse or rhythm. In other words, the music that produces is characterised by an irregular rhythm or pulse; music that can be soothing or abrasive or sparse but definitely not with a regular pulse. The torch is lusty; Lorca can't sleep, he continuously dreams of his lover. The final verses are climatic, the poison and passion of the bitter reasoning is the intellect fighting against love; reason versus love. Lorca is trying hard to be cautious, to be careful, to use his reasoning.

Lorca spent his final days carefully revising and correcting these sonnets. After the discovery of the secret box of mementoes of Ramirez de Lucas, it seems that these sonnets were addressed to him.

It is sad to think that Lorca, aged 38, was taken to a nearby hillside and was shot along with two anarchist bullfighters and a one-legged schoolteacher. His body has never been found. It is also sad to think that Ramirez de Lucas had to hide his love affair with Lorca throughout his entire life (all secretly contained in his heart and in a secret box.)

Soneto de la carta

Amor de mis entrañas, viva muerte,
En vano espero tu palabra escrita
Y pienso, con la flor que se marchita,
Que si vivo sin mí quiero perderte.

El aire es inmortal, la piedra inerte
Ni conoce la sombra ni la evita.
Corazón interior no necesita
La miel helada que la luna vierte.

Pero yo te sufrí, rasgué mis venas,
Tigre y paloma, sobre tu cintura
En duelo de mordiscos y azucenas.

Llena, pues, de palabras mi locura
O déjame vivir en mi serena
Noche del alma para siempre oscura.

Sonnet of the Letter

Love of my loins, living death. In vain,
I wait for a letter from you. And I think,
Like a withered flower, I'd rather lose you
Than live without being me.

The air is immortal, the stone lifeless
It neither knows the shade nor avoids it.
The innermost heart doesn't need the frozen
Honey pouring down from the moon.

I suffered for you. I ripped my veins.
Tiger and dove on your waist.
In a tussle of bites and lilies.

Fill now my madness with your words
Or let me live in the serene night
Of my soul, my core forever dark.

Comments on the Sonnet of the Letter

Lorca is begging his beloved to write to him. Ramirez de Lucas is the love of his loins, a love Lorca feels deeply, in Lorca's inmost self, in Lorca's depths.

Lorca's work is filled with symbolism. La luna (the moon) is one of them. La Luna vertiendo miel (the moon pouring honey) is an image that has a powerful effect, as it is a symbol of distance, presiding from high above over the feeling that Lorca has of frustration to fulfil his desire for his lover.

The tiger and the dove on the lover's waist is not a contradiction. It is simply the deep Spanish temperament of cruelty and tenderness; the ferocity of the tiger and the tenderness of the dove.

The translation into English of 'the tussle of bites and lilies' is not a tussle in the Spanish original but ' a duel' (un duelo). And again we find the word 'dark' (oscuro) in the final verse of this sonnet. "Of my soul, forever dark my core." (Siempre oscura.)

One of the first explanations of this 'darkness', or the use of the adjective 'dark', is that it refers to the homosexual nature of Lorca; Lorca is implying in this obscurity his own homosexuality.

For me, this is not the case, and the dark night, the dark soul and the dark sonnets refer to the relationship between love and secrecy. Oscuro refers to the dark and painful passion, which is either unrequited or in this case because he couldn't see his lover again, as the parents of Ramirez de Lucas wouldn't allow him.

In fact, I strongly believe that one can read Lorca without taking into account his sexuality, as his sonnets are sonnets of love, universal love that could have also been written to a woman.

El poeta dice la verdad

Quiero llorar mi pena y te lo digo
Para que tú me quieras y me llores
En un anochecer de ruiseñores
Con un puñal, con besos y contigo.

Quiero matar al único testigo
Para el asesinato de mis flores
Y convertir mi llanto y sudores
En eterno montón de duro trigo.

Que no se acabe nunca la madeja
Del te quiero me quieres, siempre ardida
Con decrépito sol y luna vieja;

Que lo que no me des y no te pida
Será para la muerte, que no deja
Ni sombra por la carne estremecida.

The poet tells the truth

I want to shed the tears of my pain and tell you
So you love me and also cry for me
In a nightfall of nightingales
With a dagger, with kisses and with you.

I want to kill the only one to witness
The assassination of my flowers
And transform my weeping and sweat
Into an eternal heap of hard wheat.

Our skein of love should never finish with
The thread of I love you and you love me,
Let it always be burnt by the decrepit sun and the
old moon.

Whatever you don't give me and I don't ask
Will be taken by death that doesn't leave
Even a shadow on erratic flesh.

Comments on the Poet tells the Truth

At the end of his days, Lorca turned to traditional forms in poetry. His last poetic work was, in fact, Sonnets of Dark Love. For a long time, before the discovery of the secret box of Ramirez de Lucas, it was believed that Lorca was inspired to write these sonnets by Rafael Rodriguez Rapun, secretary of La Barraca. La Barraca was a theatre company, which comprised young university students. It aimed to promote travelling theatre and revitalise the Spanish stage.

Lorca wrote little poetry in this last period of his life, declaring in 1936: "theatre is poetry that rises from the book and becomes human enough to talk and shout, weep and despair".

Lorca kept Huerta de San Vicente as his summer residence in Granada from 1926 to 1936. Here he wrote some of his best works: Bodas de Sangre (Blood Wedding) 1932, Yerma (1934) and his Sonnets of Dark Love, among other major works. Lorca lived in the Huerta de San Vicente in the days before his arrest.

In Lorca's desire to turn to traditional forms of poetry, his Sonnets of Dark Love are believed to have been inspired by the 16th century Spanish poet San Juan de la Cruz. Many scholars confirm that the 'dark love' is an allusion to San Juan de la Cruz's dark night of the soul.

John of the Cross (in English) was a Spanish mystic, known for his writings. He is associated with the peak of mystical Spanish literature.

One of his most important poems is the Dark Night of the Soul, considered a masterpiece of Spanish poetry both for his formal stylistic point of view and his rich symbolism. The Dark Night of the Soul represents the hardships and difficulties in reaching the light of the union with the creator.

Lorca was inspired by this masterpiece of Spanish poetry. In his sonnets he describes the painful experiences he had to endure, not in his search for God, but instead in his search of love and union with his lover.

El poeta habla por teléfono con su amor

Tu voz regó la duna de mi pecho
En la dulce cabina de madera.
Por el sur de mis pies fue primavera
Y al norte de mi frente flor de helecho.

Pino de luz por el espacio estrecho
Cantó sin alborada y sementera
Y mi llanto prendió por vez primera
Coronas de esperanza por el techo.

Dulce y lejana voz por mí vertida.
Dulce y lejana voz por mí gustada.
Lejana y dulce voz amortecida.

Lejana como oscura corza herida.
Dulce como un sollozo en la nevada.
¡Lejana y dulce en tuétano metida!

The poet talks on the telephone with his beloved

Your voice watered the dunes of my heart.
In that sweet wooden telephone booth.
To the south at my feet was spring
And north of my forehead ferns.

In that tight space, a pine tree of light
Sang without music and without sowing.
And for the first time my weeping strung
Crowns of hope on the ceiling.

Sweet and distant voice poured by me.
Sweet and distant voice savoured by me.
Distant and sweet voice fainting away from me.

Distant like a dark wounded doe,
Sweet like a sob in the snow.
Distant and sweet, encrusted in the marrow!

Comments on the Poet talks on the telephone with his beloved

Lorca's poetry is sublime, but it is not his most important work, which was produced by the impact of his own experimental techniques upon the traditional Spanish theatre. The great success of Lorca is his trilogy: La Casa de Bernarda Alba, Yerma and Bodas de Sangre. However, whether we are dealing with his poetry or his plays, surrealism and symbolism characterise all his work.

In a way, for Lorca, realism had disappeared. For Lorca the aim of the artist is 'eliminar todos los ingredientes humanos, demasiado humanos y retener solo la materia puramente artística." (Eliminate all the human ingredients, too human, and retain only the purely artistic matter.)

We can clearly see in this sonnet that the real action is only talking on the phone with his beloved, inside a sweet telephone booth, but a large number of many other sentimental actions also take place.

Mental alertness of the surroundings (the pine tree, a visual tight space), pure imagination filled with visual effects such the voice watering his heart, a wounded woe, a sob in the snow, a final climatic end when the voice fades away encrusted in the marrow. The precipitation of his verses towards the final attack is particularly Lorquian; it is the final verse that has an emotional impact upon the reader. The impact is deep to the marrow!

El poeta pregunta a su amor por 'la Ciudad Encantada' de Cuenca

¿Te gustó la ciudad que gota a gota
labró en el centro de los pinos?
¿Viste sueños y rostros y caminos
y muros de dolor que el aire azota?

¿Viste la grieta azul de luna rota
que el Júcar moja de cristal y trinos?
¿Han besado tus dedos los espinos
que coronan de amor piedra remota?

¿Te acordaste de mí cuando subías
al silencio que sufre la serpiente
prisionera de grillos y de umbrías?

¿No viste por el aire transparente
una dalia de penas y alegrías
que te mandó mi corazón caliente?

The poet asks his beloved about the "Enchanted City" of Cuenca.

Did you like the city where, drop by drop,
The water carved the heart of the pinetrees?
Did you see dreams and faces and streets?
And the wailing walls lashed by the air?

Did you see the blue crack of broken moon that
The river Júcar wets with glass and bird songs?
Were your fingers kissed by the thorns that
 Crown with love the distant stones?

Did you remember me when you went up
Into the silence that the serpent suffers,
Captive of crickets and shadows?

Did you see in the transparent air
That dahlia of sorrow and joy that
My warm heart had sent to you?

Comments on the Poet asks his beloved about the Enchanted City of Cuenca

Cuenca is a city in central Spain, also known as the Enchanted City of Cuenca. The city is characterised by its curious rocky formations, being situated in a canyon 1,500 metres above the sea. Lorca's imagination is in its best poetic element when he is writing this sonnet to his beloved, who has visited the magical city of Cuenca. Lorca's favourite settings are rural. In these settings, Lorca finds the most spontaneous artistic forms where he can express his emotions.

When Lorca visited New York in the summer of 1929, the society he came across in the Apple shocked him. He described it as: "ritmo furioso, geometría y angustia" (furious rhythm, geometry and anguish). In New York, Lorca felt that materialism and indifference to humanity were the consequences of their mechanised kind of life. For Lorca, it was the negation of all spiritual values and the opposite of what he had known in his native Andalusia. "En ninguna parte del mundo se siente como en Nueva York la ausencia total del espíritu." (In no part of the world does one feel like they do in New York, the total absence of spirit).

In his work, Lorca preserves right up to the end of his life the use of the natural elements: water, the moon, trees, thorns, serpents, etc. All are combined with striking images. Nature is used to increase the tension and dramatic moments.

Each sonnet of Sonnets of Dark Love is a miniature of the different love episodes Lorca experienced towards his beloved.

Soneto gongorino en que el poeta manda a su amor una paloma

Este pichón del Turia que te mando,
De dulces ojos y de blanca puma,
Sobre laurel de Grecia vierte y suma
Llama lenta de amor do estoy parando.

Su cándida virtud, su cuello blando,
En limo doble de caliente espuma,
Con un temblor de escarcha, perla y bruma
La ausencia de tu boca está marcando.

Pasa la mano sobre su blancura
Y verás qué nevada melodía
Esparce en copos sobre tu hermosura.

Así mi corazón de noche y día,
Preso en la cárcel del amor oscura,
Llora sin verte su melancolía.

Gongorian* Sonnet, in which the poet sends his beloved a dove

I send you this young dove from Turia
With its sweet eyes and white feathers.
Over Grecian laurels, it flames and sparks
The slow flame of love where I come to a halt.

Its candid virtue, its soft throat,
Over a double layer of mud made of hot broth.
With a tremor of pearl, mist and frost
The bird is pecking the absence of your mouth.

Pass your hand over its whiteness
And you will see the snowy melody
Scattering snowflakes over your beauty.

In this way my heart, day and night,
Incarcerated in the prison of dark love,
Cries its melancholy for not seeing you

Comments on the Gongorian* Sonnet, in which the poet sends his beloved a dove

Why is this sonnet Gongorian? Luis de Góngora y Argote (1561-1627) was a Spanish writer and lifelong rival of Francisco de Quevedo, another famous Spanish author. Both Góngora and Quevedo are considered the most prominent Spanish poets of all time. Góngora believed in 'culteranismo', also termed Gongorism and Quevedo believed in the opposite, called conceptism.

Góngora wrote numerous sonnets and created the aforementioned personal style called Gongorism (Gongorismo). Gongorismo is characterised by using as many words as possible to convey little meaning or to conceal meaning.

Quevedo was totally the opposite, being a firm believer in a witty style, word play and the use of simple vocabulary to convey multiple meanings in as few words as possible. This was termed conceptism.

Lorca was a member of the Generation of 27, a group of poets and artists who introduced symbolism, futurism and surrealism into Spanish literature. The Generation of 27 took its name from the year of the tercentenary of Gongora's death (1627). The aim of this group of artists was to revise baroque literature, which included Góngora and Quevedo's works. Lorca presented a lecture called 'la imagen poética en don Luis de Góngora' (The Poetic Image in don Luis de Góngora) in Seville in 1927.

Lorca's Gongorian sonnet, in which he sends his beloved a dove, is a tribute to one of the greatest poets of all time.

Luis de Góngora y Argote by Diego Velazquez

Ay voz secreta del amor oscuro

Ay voz secreta del amor oscuro
¡Ay balido sin lanas! ¡Ay herida!
¡Ay aguja de hiel, camelia hundida!
¡Ay corriente sin mar, ciudad sin muro!

¡Ay noche inmensa de perfil seguro,
montaña celestial de angustia erguida!
¡Ay perro en corazón, voz perseguida!
¡Silencio sin confín, lirio maduro!

Huye de mí, caliente voz de hielo,
No me quieras perder en la maleza
Donde sin fruto gimen carne y cielo.

Deja el duro marfil de mi cabeza,
Apiádate de mí, ¡rompe mi duelo!
¡Que soy amor, que soy naturaleza!

Oh Secret Voice of Dark Love

Oh secret voice of dark love!
Oh bleeting without wool! Oh wound!
Oh needle of gall, wilting camellia!
Oh current without sea, city without walls!

Oh immense night of limited outline,
Celestial mountain erected in anguish!
Oh dog in the heart, oh persecuted voice!
Silence without boundary, mature lily!

Get away from me! Hot voice of ice
Do you want to lose me into the wilds
Where flesh and sky groan fruitlessly?

Leave alone the hard ivory of my head,
Have pity on me. Rip my internal battle to shreds!
For I am love, for I am nature!

Comments on the Sonnet Oh Secret Voice of Dark Love

In this beautiful sonnet, Lorca plays with 'apparent' contradictions, constant antonyms and perceptible paradoxes. The animal bleeting has no wool and the city has no walls (the agonising lover feels unprotected and helpless, without its 'wool' or its 'walls'). The current does not have a sea (the lover does not have the beloved to love.)

Then the paradoxes seem to appear; how can the immense night have a limited outline? How can a hot voice be of ice? Is this poetic chaos? The answer to the first question is that Lorca felt dragged upwards to the celestial heights, transported to nature, which he admires, but the grandiose nature is limited, as it cannot provide him with his lover. The answer to the second question is that the voice of our lover is warm when close to us, being arousing and comforting, but cold when far away and unreachable.

The apparent chaos is remarkably organised, culminating with Lorca's sublime final verse: "For I am love, for I am nature!" (Que soy amor, que soy naturaleza.) This final verse makes us question if Lorca was a romantic, despite him not fitting easily into any category as he combines surrealism and dense symbolic poetry. Overall, however, we are inclined to describe him as a surrealist poet rather than a romantic.

El amor duerme en el pecho del poeta

Tú nunca entenderás lo que te quiero
Porque duermes en mí y estás dormido.
Yo te oculto llorando, perseguido
Por una voz de penetrante acero.

Norma que agita igual carne y lucero
Traspasa ya mi pecho dolorido
Y las turbias palabras han mordido
Las alas de tu espíritu severo.

Grupo de gente salta en los jardines
Esperando tu cuerpo y mi agonía
En caballos de luz y verdes crines.

Pero sigue durmiendo, vida mía.
¡Oye mi sangre rota en los violines!
¡Mira que nos acechan todavía!

The beloved sleeps on the poet's breast

You will never understand how much I love you,
Because you are asleep but you sleep in me.
I hide you away as I cry, being pursued
By the voice of biting iron.

The law that troubles both flesh and star
Now pierces deep into my aching heart.
And the turbid words have bitten
The wings of your severe being.

A group of people prance in the garden
Waiting for your corpse and my agony
On horses of light with green manes.

But continue to sleep, my life.
Listen to my broken blood among the violins!
Watch out! They are ready to ambush us!

Comments on the Sonnet The Beloved sleeps on the poet's breast

In technical terms, there is nothing particularly special in this sonnet: four stanzas in total, two of four lines and the other two of three lines, and in the Spanish original version eleven syllables per line, but the implications of this sonnet are enormous. This sonnet is heavily homoerotic, as Lorca seems to be becoming braver in explaining his feelings in his descriptions. In the English translation, however, some meanings are lost. When 'the lover is asleep' (dormido) in the second verse, in Spanish 'dormido' is masculine, dormida is feminine. The beloved is a man. Lorca is sleeping with a man. This would have been shocking at the time.

Sonnets of Dark Love were only shared with friends and they were lost until 1983-1984 (these dates are not certain), when they were finally published in draft form.

This sonnet in particular was too irreverent. It was only after Franco's death that Lorca's Sonnets of Dark Love and even his life and death, could be openly discussed in Spain.

Noche del amor insomne

Noche arriba los dos con luna llena,
Yo me puse a llorar y tú reías.
Tu desden era un dios, las quejas mías
Momentos y palomas en cadena.

Noche abajo los dos. Cristal de pena,
Llorabas tú por hondas lejanías.
Mi dolor era un grupo de agonías
Sobre tu débil corazón de arena.

La aurora nos unió sobre la cama,
Las bocas puestas sobre el chorro helado
De una sangre sin fin que se derrama.

Y el sol entró por el balcón cerrado
Y el coral de la vida abrió su rama
Sobre mi corazón amortajado.

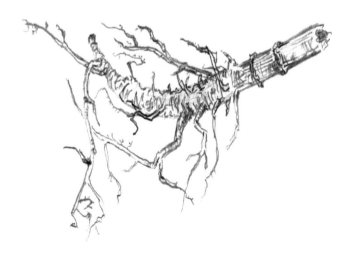

Night of Sleepless Love

Night was up, both of us under the full moon,
I began to cry and you were laughing.
Your disdain was God and my complaints
Were instants of time and chains of doves.

Night was down, both of us a crystalline pain,
You then cried for your deep remoteness.
My sorrow was a bunch of agonies,
Above your fragile heart of sand.

Dawn united us on the bed,
Our mouths were pressed on the freezing spurt
An endless stream of blood leaking out.

The sun entered through our closed balcony,
And the coral of life opened its branches
Over my shrouded heart.

Los **SONETOS DEL AMOR OSCURO** son:
"Prodigio de pasión, de entusiasmo, de felicidad, de tormento, puro y ardiente monumento al amor, en que la primera materia es ya la carne, el corazón, el alma del poeta en trance de destrucción."
Vicente Aleixandre

The Sonnets of Dark Love are…"a prodigy of passion, of enthusiasm, of happiness, of torment, a pure and ardent monument of love, in which the prime matter is the flesh, the heart, the soul of the poet, in a trance of destruction." Vicente Aleixandre

Lorca wrote two poems about farewell. One was in his Suites:

DESPEDIDA

Me despediré
en la encrucijada
para entrar en el camino
de mi alma.
Despertando recuerdos
y horas malas
llegaré al huertecillo
de mi canción blanca
y me echaré a temblar como
la estrella de la mañana.

FAREWELL

I will say good-bye
at the crossroad
to enter the path
of my soul.
Awakening memories
and bad times
I will reach the sweet orchard
of my white song
And I will tremble like
the morning star.

Another of his farewells was:

FIN

Ya pasó
el fin del mundo
y ha sido
el juicio tremendo.
Ya ocurrió catástrofe
De los luceros.

El cielo de la noche
Es un desierto,
Un desierto de lámparas
Sin dueño.

Muchedumbres de plata
Se fueron
A la densa levadura
Del misterio.

Y en el barco de la Muerte
Vamos los hombres sintiendo
Que jugamos a la vida,
¡que somos espectros!

Mirando a los cuatro puntos
Todo está muerto.
El cielo de la noche
Es una ruina,
Un eco.

THE END

It happened
The end of the world
And it was
The terrible judgement.
It occurred
The catastrophe of stars.

The night sky
Is a desert.
A desert of lamps
Without master.

Crowds of silver
Left
The dense yeast
Of mystery.

And in the boat of death
We, men, are feeling
We are playing with life,
We are spectres!

Looking at the four cardinal points
All is dead.
The night sky
Is in ruins.
An echo.

Lorca's poetic work sadly finished with his
SONNETS OF DARK LOVE. His sonnets
constitute a document of his private homosexual
passion in the classical form of the sonnet. The final
two poems that we have added come from his
SUITES, written between 1920 and 1923, and also
published after his death in 1983.

Signature of **Federico García Lorca**, from Wikipedia
https://commons.wikimedia.org/w/index.php?curid=17955291.

■ ■

Federico García Lorca was shot at 4:45 AM on the 18th August, 1936, along the path that connects Víznar to Alfacar. His body, still unfound, is most likely in a common grave somewhere along this path.

A document by the Fascist police dated in Granada on the 9th July, 1965, and discovered in 2015, indicates the reason for his execution: "mason belonging to the group 'logia Alhambra'…practised homosexuality and other aberrations."

■ ■

It seems that Lorca knew his own destiny. A
fragment of his work "Poet in New York' 1929,
reads:

Cuando se hundieron las formas puras
bajo el cri cri de las margaritas,
comprendí que me habían asesinado.
(I understood they had killed me.)

Recorrieron los cafés y los cementerios y las
iglesias,
abrieron los toneles y los armarios,
destrozaron tres esqueletos para arrancar sus dientes
de oro.

Ya no me encontraron.
(And they never found me.)
¿No me encontraron?
(They never found me?)
No. No me encontraron.
(No, they never found me)

Pero se supo que la sexta luna huyó torrente arriba,
y que el mar recordó ¡de pronto!
los nombres de todos sus ahogados.

Fragmento de la "Fábula y rueda de tres amigos"
Poeta en Nueva York.

'Sonnets of Dark Love' with parallel Spanish text is our little homage to Federico García LORCA. These sonnets, and three other selected poems from his Suites and Poet in New York, come with vintage images in our attempt to combine the elegant and delicate poetry of Lorca with visual effects. We hope you enjoy this work of dark love as much as we have enjoyed these masterpieces of Spanish poetry.

We offer the following literary works on Amazon:

Don Quixote, a
Journey with Pictures
Miguel De Cervantes

Julio Romero
de Torres

Julio Viernes

JULIO ROMERO DE TORRES The Famous Spanish
Painter who painted dark-skinned women El Famoso
Pintor Español que pintaba mujeres morenas This
bilingual edition (English and Spanish) includes the most
famous paintings of Julio Romero de Torres, together
with the lyrics of some Spanish songs with parallel
English texts. This is our little homage to Julio Romero de
Torres, one of the most iconic Spanish painters.

The Rubaiyat of Omar Khayyam, also translated by Mar Escribano into Spanish from the English version of Edward FitzGerald. (With images.)

Learn English with the Erotic Alphabet (Aprende inglés con el alfabeto erótico.)

Your task is to turn the pages of this Happy St. Valentine's Day Book and discover, in Black and White, the hidden treasures in the love quotes from the past. This is a book full of beautiful black and white vintage images. Please take a step back in time and feel free to travel with your imagination. And don't forget: HAPPY ST. VALENTINE'S DAY!!!!!

You can visit us on Amazon if you wish

https://www.amazon.co.uk/Julio-
Viernes/e/B078Q6HYHR/ref=dp_byline_cont_book_1

Or: https://www.amazon.co.uk/Mar-
Escribano/e/B00VIA852Q/ref=sr_tc_2_0?qid=152129188
1&sr=1-2-ent

You can also contact us via the email:

margalianescribano@gmail.com

Made in the USA
Middletown, DE
19 January 2025

69812231R00035